Mc
Graw
Hill
Education

Cover and Title Page: Nathan Love

www.mheonline.com/readingwonders

Send all inquiries to:
McGraw-Hill Education
2 Penn Plaza
New York, NY 10121

ISBN: 978-0-02-132756-0
MHID: 0-02-132756-4

Printed in the United States of America

2 3 4 5 6 7 8 9 RMN 20 19 18 17 16

ELD
Companion Worktext

Program Authors

Diane August

Jana Echevarria

Josefina V. Tinajero

McGraw Hill Education

Unit 6

Think It Over

The Big Idea

Unit 6

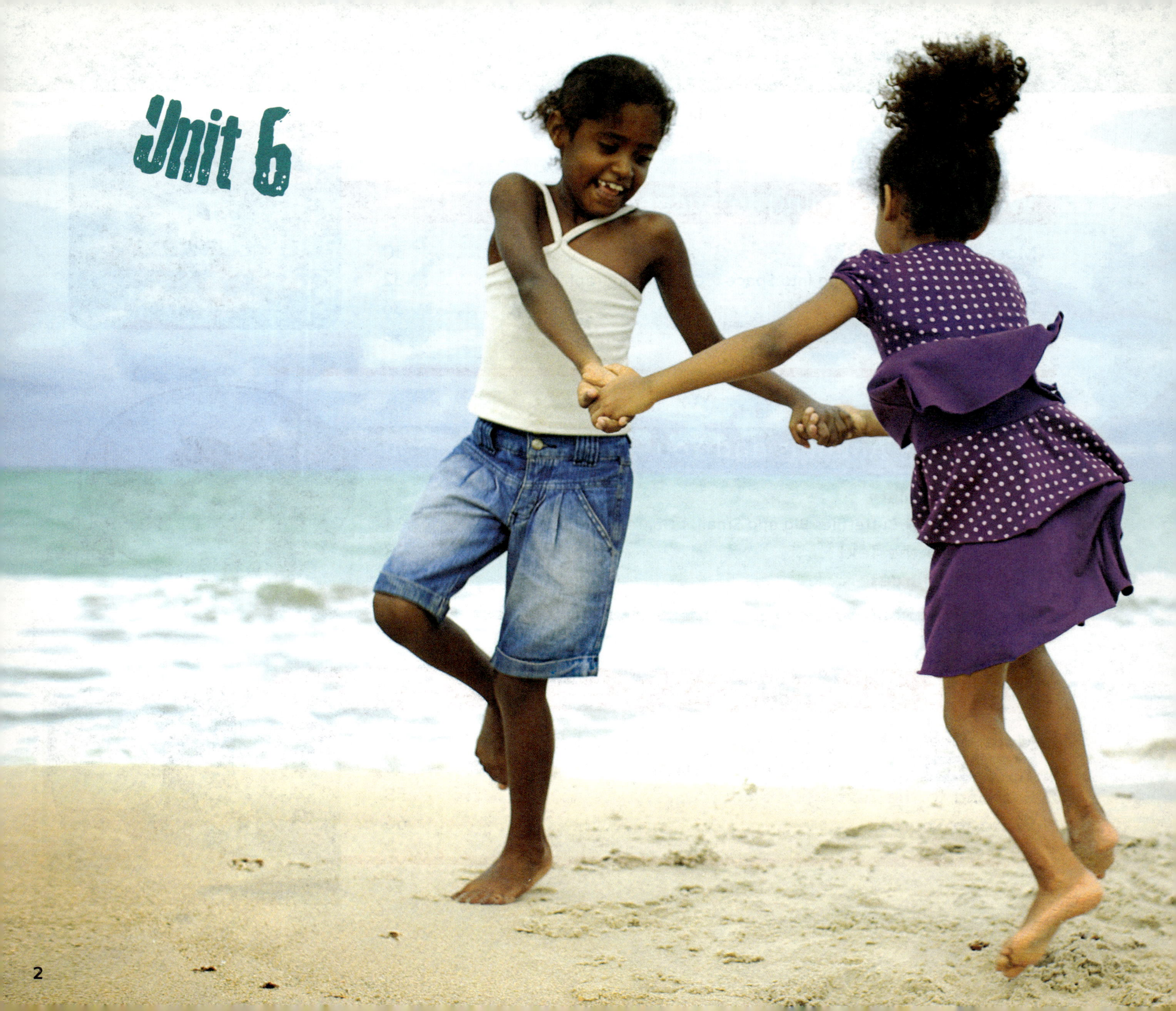

Think It Over

The BiG Idea

How do we decide what's important?

TALK ABOUT IT

Weekly Concept Treasures

? Essential Question
How do you decide
what's important?

>> *Go Digital*

COLLABORATE

What is the girl doing? Who is important to her? What does she value? Write the words in the web.

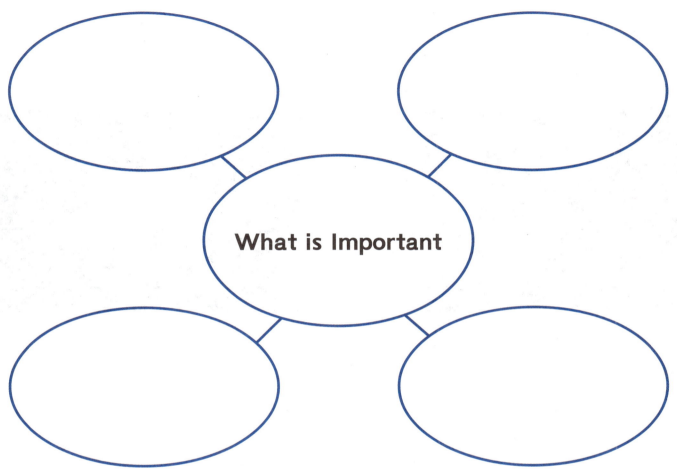

What is Important

Discuss what the girl and her grandfather are doing. Talk about what is important to her. Use the words from the web. You can say:

The girl likes _____ with her _____.

Spending time with _____ is important to her.

_____ is important to her.

More Vocabulary

Look at the picture and read the word. Then read the sentences.
Talk about the word with a partner. Write your own sentence.

afford

Donna can **afford** to buy a teddy bear.

Complete the sentence. Write the word.

Can you _____ **a new toy?**

What toy can you afford?

I can afford _____

_____.

possession

This baseball is my favorite **possession**.

What phrase means *possession*?

**something you own   a special gift
a notebook**

What is your favorite possession?

My favorite possession is _____

_____.

Words and Phrases: Homophones *you're* and *your*

The word *you're* is a contraction of *you are*.

Who is coming with us?

You're coming with us.

The word *your* means "belonging to you."

Whose folder is this?

This is **your** folder.

COLLABORATE

Talk with a partner. Look at the pictures. Read the sentences. Write the word that completes the sentence.

Here is _____ lunch.

you're   your

_____ a good artist.

You're   Your

COLLABORATE

1 Talk About It

Look at the picture. Read the title. Discuss what you see. Use these words.

Athena   Arachne

cloth   weaving

Write about what you see.

The play is about _____

_____.

What are the women doing?

They are _____

_____.

Take notes as you read the drama.

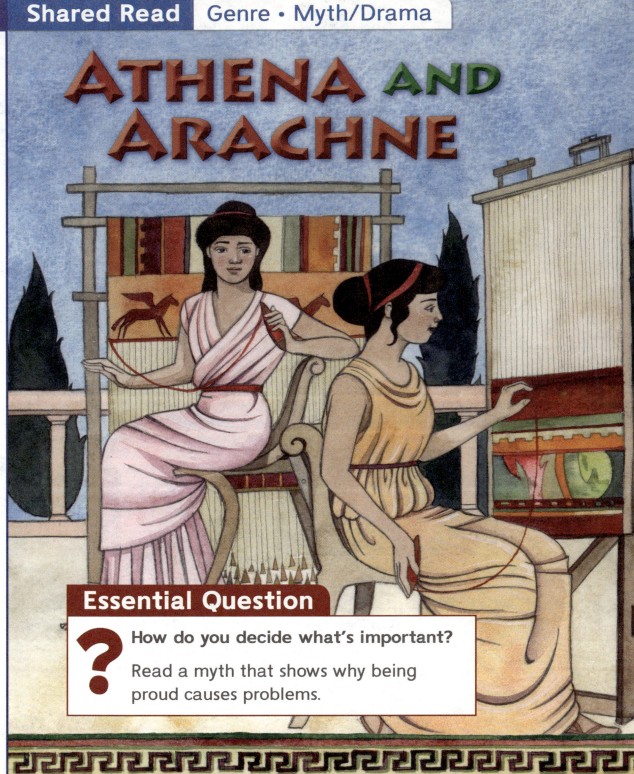

ATHENA AND ARACHNE

Essential Question

? How do you decide what's important?

Read a myth that shows why being proud causes problems.

CHARACTERS

NARRATOR

ARACHNE (uh-RAK-nee)

DIANA: Arachne's friend

ATHENA: a Greek goddess

MESSENGER

⇒ SCENE ONE ⇐

Athens, Greece, a long time ago.

NARRATOR: Long ago, Arachne and her friend Diana were weaving.

DIANA: Arachne, that cloth is so beautiful!

Arachne admires her cloth.

ARACHNE: I know. Many people want to buy my cloth. But most people cannot **afford** it.

DIANA: Many people love your weaving. It is one of their most valued **possessions**. Some people say that the goddess Athena taught you how to weave.

ARACHNE: I did not need weaving lessons from a goddess. I was born with a **talent** to weave. And I am a much better weaver than Athena. I am sure I can win a weaving contest with her!

DIANA: Ssshhh! I hope Athena isn't listening, or you're in trouble!

ARACHNE: Don't worry. Athena is too busy to leave Mount Olympus. She will not compete with me.

Jenny Reynish

Text Evidence

❶ Sentence Structure Ⓐ Ⓒ Ⓣ

Who speaks first in this play? Underline the word that tells you who is speaking.

❷ Specific Vocabulary Ⓐ Ⓒ Ⓣ

A *talent* is a natural ability or skill. What is Arachne's talent?

Arachne's talent is _____

_____.

COLLABORATE

❸ Talk About It

Why does Arachne think she can beat Athena in a weaving contest? Justify your answer.

Arachne thinks she can beat

Athena because _____

_____

_____.

9

Text Evidence

1 Sentence Structure ACT

Reread the last sentence in Scene Two. Circle the connecting word that joins the two parts of the sentence. What will happen if Arachne does not apologize? Underline the part of the sentence that tells you.

2 Specific Vocabulary ACT

Read the last sentence in Scene Two. A *boastful* person is proud and likes to brag. Why is Arachne boastful?

Arachne is boastful because she

_____ .

COLLABORATE

3 Talk About It

Why is Athena angry? Discuss with a partner.

Athena is _____

_____ .

10

⤖ SCENE TWO ⤖

Mount Olympus, home of Athena. A messenger arrives.

MESSENGER: Goddess Athena! I have news from Athens. The weaver Arachne says that she can beat you in a weaving contest.

ATHENA: I will show her that I weave the finest cloth! Please get me my cloak. *Messenger gives Athena her cloak.*

ATHENA: Arachne cannot say mean things about me! She has to apologize, or I will make her pay for her boastful words.

⤖ SCENE THREE ⤖

Arachne's home. There is a knock at the door.

ARACHNE: Who is there?

ATHENA: I am an old woman, and I have a question.

Athena is hiding under her cloak. She enters the room.

ATHENA: Is it true that you want to compete with the goddess Athena?

ARACHNE: Yes, that's right. *Athena drops her cloak.*

ATHENA: Well, I am Athena. And I am here to compete in a weaving contest with you!

DIANA: Arachne, please do not compete with the goddess Athena! It is not a good idea.

Arachne and Athena begin to weave furiously.

NARRATOR: Arachne and Athena both wove beautiful cloths. However, Arachne's cloth was filled with unkind pictures about the gods.

ATHENA: Arachne, your weaving is beautiful, but I am **insulted**. Your cloth is mean and unkind. As a result, I will punish you.

Athena points at Arachne. Arachne falls behind her loom and crawls out as a spider.

ATHENA: Arachne, you will spend the rest of your life weaving and living in your own web.

NARRATOR: Arachne was mean and boastful, so Athena turned her into a spider. That is why spiders are called arachnids. Arachne learned that bragging and too much pride can lead to trouble.

⇒ **THE END** ⇐

Jenny Reynish

Make Connections

What does Arachne value? How does it cause her trouble? **ESSENTIAL QUESTION**

What do you value? Why do you value it? **TEXT TO SELF**

1 Specific Vocabulary A C T

When you *insult* someone, you do or say something rude. How does Arachne insult Athena? Underline the words that tell you.

2 Sentence Structure A C T

Look at the second sentence of the stage direction. Circle the subject. Underline the two actions. Draw a box around the word that connects the two actions.

3 Comprehension
Theme

The theme of a drama is the author's message. Think about what the characters do and say in *Athena and Arachne*. What is the theme of this drama? Underline the sentence on this page that tells the theme.

Respond to the Text

Partner Discussion Work with a partner. Read the questions about "Athena and Arachne." Show where you found text evidence. Write page numbers. Then discuss what you learned.

How does Arachne feel about her talent?

Arachne's cloth is _____.

Arachne says she was born _____.

Arachne tells Diana that she can beat Athena in a _____.

Text Evidence 🔍

Page(s): _____

Page(s): _____

Page(s): _____

How does Arachne's talent cause her a problem?

I read that Athena wants a weaving contest with _____.

Arachne's weaving is _____, but her pictures are

_____.

I read that Athena turns Arachne into a _____.

Text Evidence 🔍

Page(s): _____

Page(s): _____

Page(s): _____

Group Discussion Present your answers to the class. Cite text evidence for your ideas. Listen to and discuss the group's opinions.

Write Work with a partner. Look at your notes about "Athena and Arachne." Write your answer to the Essential Question. Use text evidence to support your answer. Use vocabulary words in your writing.

Why does Arachne's talent cause a problem for her?

Arachne tells Diana _____.

Athena is angry and _____.

Athena and Arachne compete in a _____

_____.

Then Athena turns _____ into a

_____ because

_____

_____.

Share Writing Present your writing to the class. Discuss their opinions. Think about their ideas. Explain why you agree or disagree. You can say:

I think your ideas are _____.

I do not agree because _____.

pages 8–11

Holly

Take Notes About the Text I took notes about the play on this chart to answer the prompt: *Athena turned Arachne into a spider. Do you think this was fair? Give reasons from the text to support your opinion.*

Arachne said she was a better weaver than Athena.

↓

Athena came to compete with Arachne.

↓

Arachne wove a cloth with unkind pictures.

↓

Athena turned Arachne into a spider.

Write About the Text I used my notes to write about Athena turning Arachne into a spider.

Student Model: *Opinion*

Athena turned Arachne into a spider. I do not think it was fair. Arachne was boastful. Arachne was unkind. Arachne said she was a better weaver than Athena. Arachne and Athena had a weaving contest. Arachne wove a cloth with unkind pictures. So Athena turned Arachne into a spider. But this act was very unkind. Now Arachne cannot talk to her friends. She cannot have fun. She is just a spider. This is not fair.

TALK ABOUT IT

Text Evidence
Underline the last sentence. Where else does Holly write that it wasn't nice for Athena to turn Arachne into a spider?

Grammar
Circle the sentence with the words *just a spider*. Add an adjective to the sentence.

Condense Ideas
Draw a box around sentences three and four. How can you condense the two sentences to make one detailed sentence?

Your Turn

Is Diana or Arachne a better friend? Use reasons from the text to support your opinion.

>> *Go Digital*
Write your response online. Use your editing checklist.

TALK ABOUT IT

Weekly Concept Weather

? **Essential Question**
How can weather affect us?

>> *Go Digital*

COLLABORATE

Look at the picture. What are the kids doing? How is weather affecting them? Write the words in the web.

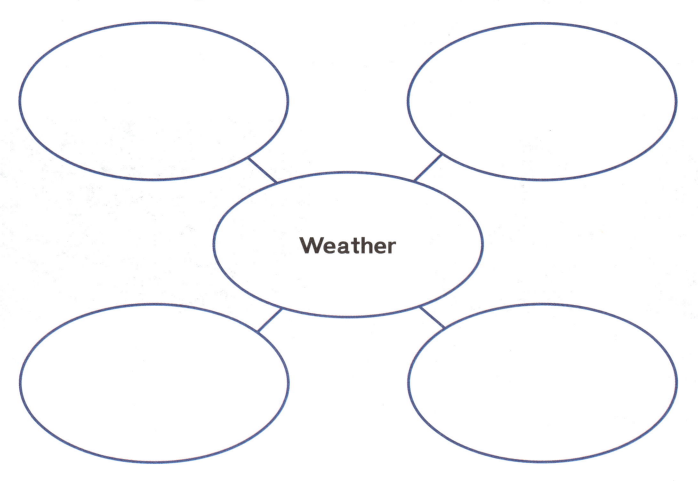

Weather

Discuss what the kids are doing. Talk about how the weather is affecting them. Use the words from the web. You can say:

It is _____ outside.

The kids put on their_____ and _____.

They are _____ in the rain.

More Vocabulary

Look at the picture and read the word. Then read the sentences. Talk about the word with a partner. Write your own sentence.

dangerous

Riding without a helmet is **dangerous**.

What word means the opposite of *dangerous?*

safe   **not safe**

What can be dangerous?

It can be dangerous to _____

_____.

unable

The cat is **unable** to go inside.

What word means the opposite of *unable?*

happy   **able**   **bad**

What is something you are unable to do?

I am unable to _____

_____

_____.

Words and Phrases: Phrasal Verbs

The phrasal verb *make it* means "go someplace."

Will the woman climb to the top?

Yes, she will **make it** to the top.

The phrasal verb *stuck at* means "not able to leave someplace."

Why is the boy inside?

He is **stuck at** home.

 Talk with a partner. Look at the pictures. Read the sentences. Write the words that complete the sentence.

We were _____ home during a big storm.

make it   **stuck at**

We will _____ to the park for a picnic.

make it   **stuck at**

(tl)Image Source; (tr)SolStock/iStock/Getty Images Plus; (bl)WeatherVideoHD.TV; (br)Juice Images/Alamy

COLLABORATE

1 **Talk About It**

Look at the picture. Then read the title. Discuss what you see. Use these words.

blizzard radio listen worried

Write about what you see.

The story is about a _____

_____.

Who are the characters?

The characters are _____

_____.

What are their feelings?

They feel _____

_____.

Take notes as you read the story.

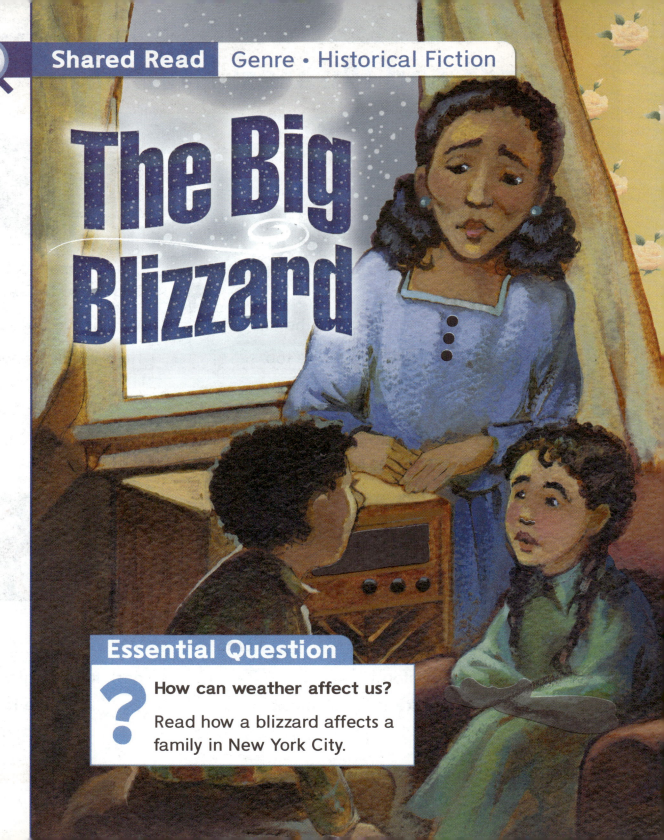

The Big Blizzard

Essential Question

? How can weather affect us?

Read how a blizzard affects a family in New York City.

20

It was a winter day in 1947 in New York City. Rosa and Eddie listened to the radio. The radio announcer discussed the terrible **blizzard**.

"This blizzard is the biggest snowstorm in our city's history! It caused the subway system to stop yesterday. It is very **dangerous**. Parents will not let their children go outside. Today the weather forecast predicts that the snow will stop. The mayor has a message to all New Yorkers: Help each other in this disaster."

"When will Papá get home from work?" whispered Rosa. She felt worried.

"He must be stuck at work and is **unable** to get home," Mamá said. "But don't worry. The snow is stopping now. I'm sure he will make it home soon."

Mamá went into the kitchen to make lunch. She returned and was carrying her coat and scarf.

"We are out of milk and bread. I need to go to Maria's Market," said Mamá.

Rosa and Eddie begged to go with her. They spent two days indoors because it was snowing so hard.

Text Evidence

1 **Sentence Structure** A C T

Reread the first sentence. Which words tell when the story takes place? Underline them. Which words tell where the story takes place? Circle them.

2 **Specific Vocabulary** A C T

Look at the word *blizzard.* Write the words in the next sentence that tell what a blizzard is.

A blizzard is _____.

COLLABORATE

3 **Talk About It**

Why is Mamá going outside into the snow? Why do Rosa and Eddie want to go out?

Mamá needs to go to _____

_____.

Rosa and Eddie want to _____

_____.

Text Evidence

1 Sentence Structure **A C T**

Reread the first sentence in paragraph four. Circle the past-tense verb. What is the family doing? Write the verb.

_____

2 Specific Vocabulary **A C T**

Look at the last sentence. The idiom *give someone a hand* means "to help someone." Why does Rosa want to give Maria a hand?

Rosa wants to _____

because _____.

COLLABORATE

3 Talk About It

How are Rosa, Eddie, and Mamá helpful? Justify your answer.

_____

_____

_____

"Okay," said Mamá. "But we have to stay close to each other."

Rosa, Eddie, and Mamá walked outside. They saw a huge wall of snow. It was higher than Rosa's head! Then their neighbor Mr. Colón arrived with two shovels.

"Who wants to help me shovel the snow?" he asked.

The family shoveled snow off of the sidewalk. It was hard work. Rosa and Eddie finished the job, and then they looked across the street. Snow still covered the sidewalk in front of Maria's Market. Maria, the owner, was trying to sweep away the snow with a small broom.

"Mr. Colón, may we borrow your shovels?" asked Rosa. "I want to **give Maria a hand**."

Shoveling Maria's walk was **a piece of cake** for Rosa and Eddie. It was easy. Then Maria gave Mamá milk and bread to thank them.

As Rosa and Eddie crossed the snowy street with Mamá, they heard a familiar voice.

"Is that my Rosa and Eddie?"

"Papá!" they shouted. Rosa told Papá about how they helped Mr. Colón and Maria.

"I'm happy to finally be home," said Papá. "And I am very proud of you because you helped our neighbors."

Make Connections

? How does weather affect the family? **ESSENTIAL QUESTION**

Think about a time when the weather was bad. What did you or your family do to help someone? **TEXT TO SELF**

Stacey Schuett

Text Evidence

1 Specific Vocabulary Ⓐ Ⓒ Ⓣ

Circle the idiom *a piece of cake*. It means "easy to do." What was a piece of cake? Underline the words.

2 Sentence Structure Ⓐ Ⓒ Ⓣ

Read the second paragraph. The connecting word *as* shows that two things are happening at the same time. Circle *as*. Underline the two things that are happening at the same time.

3 Comprehension

Theme

Reread the mayor's message to the city in paragraph two on page 21. It tells the theme of the story. What details in paragraphs one and four support the theme? Write the details.

_____

_____

_____

Respond to the Text

COLLABORATE

Partner Discussion Work with a partner. Read the questions about "The Big Blizzard." Show where you found text evidence. Write the page numbers. Then discuss what you learned.

How does the blizzard affect New York City?

In the story, the mayor tells New Yorkers to _____.

I read that Papá is stuck _____.

Rosa and Eddie are inside _____ because

_____.

Text Evidence 🔍

Page(s): _____

Page(s): _____

Page(s): _____

How do the neighbors help each other?

I read that Mr. Colón helps neighbors by _____.

In the story, Rosa and Eddie help Mrs. Sanchez _____.

Mrs. Sanchez gives Mamá _____ because

_____.

Text Evidence 🔍

Page(s): _____

Page(s): _____

Page(s): _____

COLLABORATE

Group Discussion Present your answers to the class. Cite text evidence for your ideas. Listen to and discuss the group's opinions.

Write Work with a partner. Look at your notes about "The Big Blizzard." Write your answer to the Essential Question. Use text evidence to support your answer. Use vocabulary words in your writing.

How does the weather affect Rosa, Eddie, and Mamá?

In New York City, a _____ causes Papá _____.

Then Rosa, Eddie and Mamá go outside to _____.

Rosa and Eddie help _____

_____.

Mrs. Sanchez gives the family _____ because

_____.

Papá is proud of Rosa and Eddie because _____.

Share Writing Present your writing to the class. Then talk about their opinions. Think about their ideas. Explain why you agree or disagree with their ideas. You can say:

I agree with _____.

That's a good comment, but _____.

pages 20-23

Harrison

Take Notes About the Text I took notes on this chart to respond to the prompt: *Write a letter from Rosa to her Grandma about the blizzard. Use details from the text.*

Rosa and Eddie stayed inside for two days.

↓

Rosa and Eddie went out with Mamá.

↓

Rosa and Eddie helped shovel snow.

↓

Papá was at work, but then he came home.

Write About the Text I used notes from my chart to write a letter from Rosa to her Grandma.

Student Model: *Narrative Text*

Dear Grandma,

Last week was so much fun! We stayed inside for two days. There was a blizzard. Papá was at work, and we were worried. Mamá needed to go to the store so Eddie and I went with her. The snow was higher than my head! Eddie and I helped shovel snow. And then Papá came home! We were happy to see him. It was a great day!

Love,

Rosa

TALK ABOUT IT

Text Evidence

Circle the last sentence. Where else does Rosa mention that she was happy or had fun? **Underline** those sentences.

Grammar

Underline the sixth sentence. **Circle** the two things that are being compared.

Connect Ideas

Draw a box around the second and third sentences. How can you connect the ideas with the word *because*?

Your Turn

Write a letter from Mamá to her friend Rita. Tell what the family did when they went outside.

>> *Go Digital*
Write your response online. Use your editing checklist.

Weekly Concept Learning to Succeed

? **Essential Question**
Why are goals important?

» *Go Digital*

COLLABORATE

Look at the picture. Why is the girl raising her arms? How did she reach her goal? Write the words in the web.

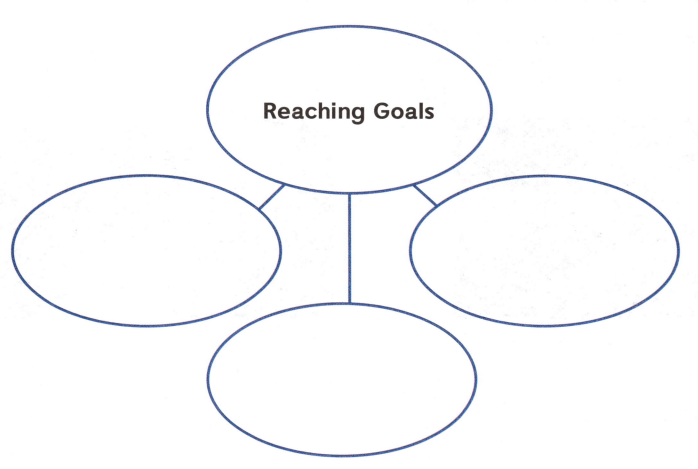

Reaching Goals

Discuss how we reach our goals. Talk about how it feels to reach a goal. Use the words from the web. You can say:

We _____ to reach our goals.

We _____ our best.

It feels _____ to reach a goal.

More Vocabulary

Look at the picture and read the word. Then read the sentences. Talk about the word with a partner. Write your own sentence.

COLLABORATE

allowed

We **allowed** Rex to sleep on the couch.

What word means *allowed*?

ran   beside   let

What is something you are allowed to do?

I am allowed to _____

_____.

favorite

Her **favorite** animal is the cat.

Complete the sentence. Write the word.

Seeds are the bird's _____ food.

What is your favorite food?

My favorite food is _____

_____.

(l)Ingram Publishing; (r)Lynn Koenig/Getty Images

Words and Phrases: Phrasal Verbs

The phrasal verb *grow up* means to grow from a child into an adult.

What will he grow up to be?

He will **grow up** to be a chef.

The phrasal verb *get back* means to return to a place.

How will they return to school?

They will **get back** to school on the bus.

Talk with a partner. Look at the pictures. Read the sentences. Write the words that complete the sentence.

He will take a cab to _____ home.

grow up   get back

She wants to be a singer when she

_____.

grows up   gets back

COLLABORATE

1 Talk About It

Look at the photograph. Read the title. Discuss what you see. Use these words.

astronaut space rocket

Write about what you see.

The text is about _____

_____

_____.

What was the man's job?

The man was an _____

_____.

Where did the man go?

The man went _____

_____.

Take notes as you read the text.

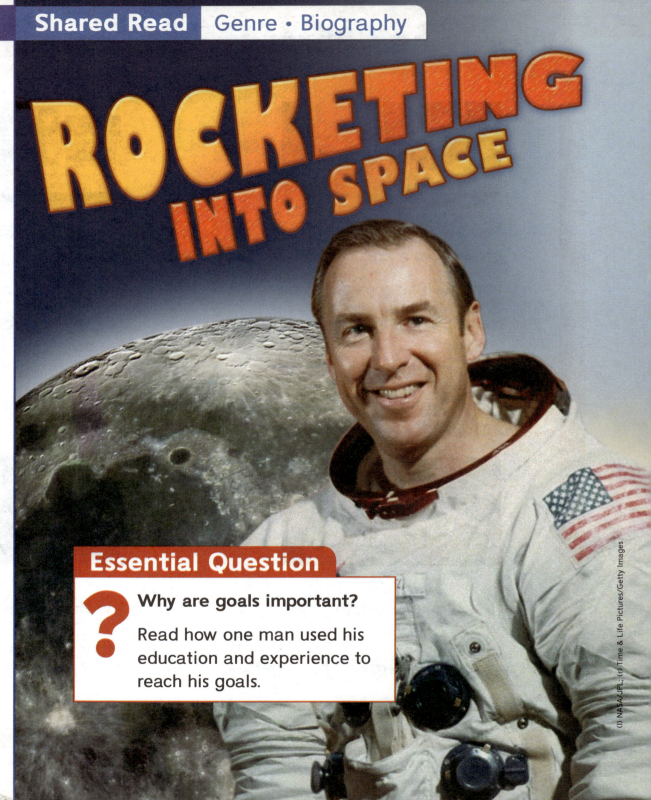

ROCKETING INTO SPACE

Essential Question

?   **Why are goals important?**

Read how one man used his education and experience to reach his goals.

(l) NASA/JPL, (r) Time & Life Pictures/Getty Images

James A. Lovell, Jr. loved to build rockets when he was a boy. He also liked to **launch** them into the sky. Lovell was like many boys who grew up in the 1930s. He wanted to be a pilot.

HIGH FLYING DREAMS

Lovell was born in Cleveland, Ohio, in 1928. He worked hard in school and planned to go to a special college. He wanted to study rockets. Unfortunately, he didn't have enough money to go to the special college. But he was motivated to find a way to fly rockets.

Lovell went to college near his home for two years. Then he signed up for flight training at the U.S. Naval Academy. After four years, Lovell joined the U.S. Navy and became a professional naval test pilot. His job was to fly planes before any other pilots were **allowed** to fly them.

NASA

James A. Lovell, Jr. became an astronaut in 1962. He flew four space missions.

1 Specific Vocabulary Ⓐ Ⓒ Ⓣ

Look at the first two sentences. The word *launch* means "to send something into space." What did James Lovell love to launch? Circle the word.

2 Sentence Structure Ⓐ Ⓒ Ⓣ

Reread the third sentence in the third paragraph. Draw a box around the phrase that tells when Lovell joined the U.S. Navy.

COLLABORATE

3 Talk About It

How did James Lovell find a way to fly rockets?

James Lovell went to college

and _____.

He became a Navy test pilot and

_____

_____.

33

Text Evidence

1 Specific Vocabulary Ⓐ Ⓒ Ⓣ

Read the fourth sentence in the first paragraph. The word *applied* means "asked for something." Why did Lovell apply for the job at NASA? Underline the words that tell you.

2 Comprehension
Problem and Solution

Look at the third paragraph. Which sentence tells the problem that the Apollo 13 astronauts had? Circle the sentence.

3 Sentence Structure Ⓐ Ⓒ Ⓣ

Reread the fourth sentence in the last paragraph. Circle the commas. Underline the name of each item. Draw a box around the subject of the sentence. Who is the subject? Write it below.

The subject is _____.

PILOT TO ASTRONAUT

Lovell taught other pilots how to fly. He worked in air flight safety. Soon, NASA asked for astronauts. Lovell **applied** for the job because he had the skills needed to fly into space. In 1962, NASA chose him, and James Lovell finally reached his goal of becoming an astronaut.

BIG CHALLENGES

Lovell flew on three space missions. Then, in 1970, Lovell became commander of the Apollo 13 space mission. This was a big challenge for Lovell.

NASA wanted Apollo 13 to land on the Moon. But the spaceship had a problem two days after it left Earth.

One of its oxygen tanks exploded, and the crew did not have enough air to breathe.

No one knew what to do. Then the team at NASA thought of a solution. The astronauts followed NASA's directions. They built an invention using plastic bags, cardboard, and tape. It worked! It cleaned the air in the spacecraft. But the next problem was bigger. How were the astronauts going to get back to Earth?

NASA's team works to solve Apollo 13's problem.

A JOB WELL DONE

The NASA team asked the astronauts to use the **lunar**, or moon, module as a lifeboat. The astronauts climbed into the module and moved away from the main spaceship.

The trip back to Earth was dangerous and scary. The astronauts traveled for almost four days. They were cold, thirsty, and hungry. Millions of people watched on television as the module fell to Earth.

Years later, James Lovell talked about Apollo 13. He told about his **favorite** memory. He knew he was safe when the module splashed down in the ocean.

The Apollo 13 crew splashed down safely on April 17, 1970.

(bkgd) NASA; (i) ©Bettmann/Corbis

A Dream Come True

DO YOU DREAM OF GOING INTO SPACE? CHECK OUT SPACE CAMP!

Space camps are more than 30 years old. They make science, math, and technology exciting for kids. Then kids want to learn. These camps are like the NASA training programs. They teach that teamwork and leadership are important.

Make Connections

? How did James Lovell's childhood goals help him as an adult? ESSENTIAL QUESTION

Tell about one of your goals. What can you do to achieve it? TEXT TO SELF

Text Evidence

1 Specific Vocabulary Ⓐ Ⓒ Ⓣ

Reread the sentence with the word *lunar*. What other words in the sentence give clues about the meaning of *lunar*? Write the meaning.

Lunar means _____.

2 Sentence Structure Ⓐ Ⓒ Ⓣ

Look at the last sentence of the second paragraph. The word *as* shows that two events are happening at the same time. Circle the word *as*. Underline the two things that happened at the same time.

COLLABORATE

3 Talk About It

How are space camps like NASA training programs? Justify your answer.

Space camps and the training programs both _____

_____.

35

Respond to the Text

Partner Discussion Work with a partner. Read the questions about "Rocketing Into Space." Show where you found text evidence. Write the page numbers. Then discuss what you learned.

What were James A. Lovell, Jr.'s goals?

I read that Lovell dreamed of _____ when he was a

_____.

In the text, Lovell was motivated to _____.

Text Evidence 🔍

Page(s): _____

Page(s): _____

What did Lovell do before he was an astronaut?

In the text, Lovell went to college and then _____

_____.

The author says that Lovell taught _____.

I read that Lovell worked in _____.

In 1962, NASA chose him to become _____ because

_____.

Text Evidence 🔍

Page(s): _____

Page(s): _____

Page(s): _____

Page(s): _____

Group Discussion Present your answers to the group. Cite text evidence for your ideas. Listen to and discuss the group's opinions.

Write Work with a partner. Look at your notes about "Rocketing Into Space." Write your answer to the Essential Question. Use text evidence to support your answer. Use vocabulary words in your writing.

> **Why were James A. Lovell, Jr.'s goals important?**
>
> First, Lovell decided he wanted to _____
>
> _____.
>
> But Lovell did not have enough _____ to
>
> _____ so he
>
> _____.
>
> Then, Lovell joined the U.S. Navy to _____
>
> _____.
>
> Finally, NASA chose Lovell to become _____ because _____
>
> _____.

Share Writing Present your writing to the class. Then talk about their opinions. Think about their ideas. Explain why you agree or disagree with their ideas. You can say:

I think your idea is _____.

I do not agree because _____.

Write to Sources

pages 32–35

Take Notes About the Text I took notes about the text on this chart to answer the question: *How did working hard help James Lovell reach his goal? Use text evidence to support your answer.*

Yusuf

Lovell went to college for two years.

⬇

Next, he went to the Naval Academy for flight training.

⬇

He joined the U.S. Navy and became a test pilot.

⬇

He became an astronaut with NASA in 1962.

Write About the Text I used notes to write about how James Lovell worked hard to reach his goal.

Student Model: *Informative Text*

James Lovell wanted to be an astronaut, and he worked hard to reach his goal. First, Lovell went to college for two years. Next, he went to the Naval Academy for flight training. After that, he joined the U.S. Navy. He became a test pilot. Later Lovell joined NASA. Lovell became an astronaut! His hard work helped him reach his goal.

TALK ABOUT IT

Text Evidence
Draw a box around the sentence about Lovell going to college. What word does Yusuf use to tell when this happened?

Grammar
Circle the seventh sentence. What detail can you add to the sentence that tells when?

Condense Ideas
Underline the fourth and fifth sentences. How can you combine the sentences into one detailed sentence?

Your Turn
What was the first problem the Apollo 13 mission had? How did the NASA team solve it? Use text evidence.

>> *Go Digital*
Write your response online. Use your editing checklist.

TALK ABOUT IT

Weekly Concept Animals and You

? Essential Question
How can learning about animals help you respect them?

>> Go Digital

40

COLLABORATE

Look at the picture. What animal is the girl learning about? What is she doing with the animal? Write the words in the web.

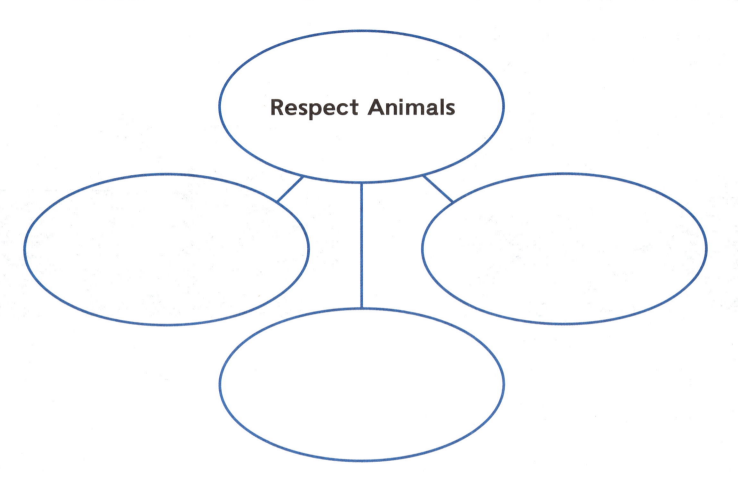

Respect Animals

Discuss how the girl is learning about animals. Talk about how she is respecting them. Use the words from the web. You can say:

The girl is learning how to treat an _____.

She uses a glove to _____ the owl.

She is learning how to _____ it.

More Vocabulary

COLLABORATE

Look at the picture and read the word. Then read the sentences.
Talk about the word with a partner. Write your own sentence.

future

Cities in the **future** will look like this city.

What word means the opposite of *future*?

next   past   present

What is something you will do in the future?

I will _____

_____

_____ in the future.

preserve

National parks **preserve** land and animals.

What word means *preserve*?

harm   like   protect

What is something you would like to preserve?

I would like to preserve _____

_____

_____.

42

(l)Andy Brandl/Moment/Getty Images; (r)NPS photo by Jim Peaco

Words and Phrases: Comparative endings *-er* and *-est*

The ending *-er* can mean "more." It is used when comparing two people or things.

Who is shorter?

The boy is **short**<mark>er</mark> than his brother.

The ending *-est* can mean "most." It is used when comparing one person or thing to others.

Who is the shortest person in the photograph?

The boy is the **short**<mark>est</mark>.

 Talk with a partner. Look at the pictures. Read the sentences. Write the words that complete the sentence.

The hen is _____ than her chicks.

bigger   **biggest**

The dog is the _____ of the three pets.

bigger   **biggest**

1 Talk About It

Look at the photograph. Read the title. Discuss what you see. Use these words.

tree butterflies sitting colorful

Write about what you see.

The text is about _____

_____.

What are the butterflies doing?

The butterflies _____

_____.

Describe how the butterflies look.

The butterflies look _____

_____.

Take notes as you read the text.

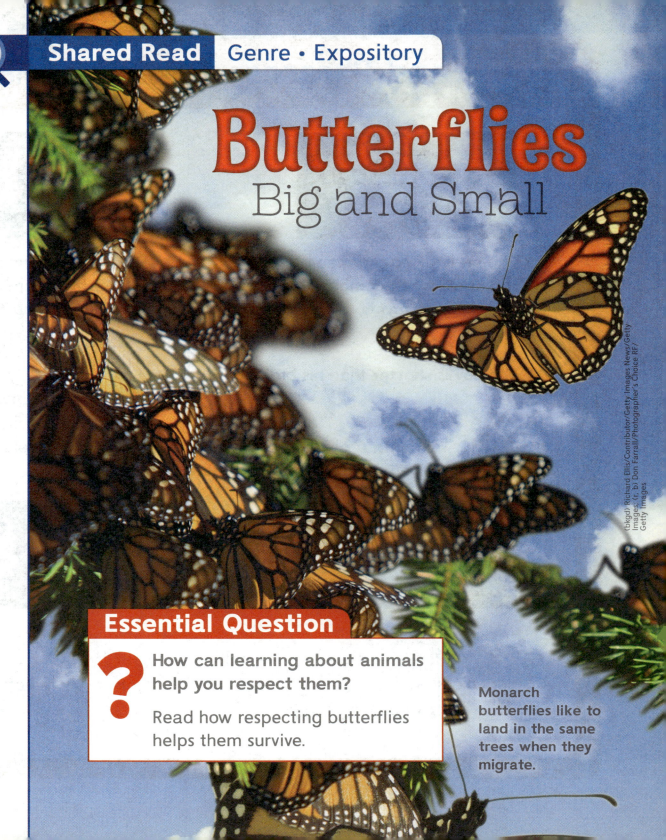

Butterflies
Big and Small

Essential Question

? How can learning about animals help you respect them?

Read how respecting butterflies helps them survive.

Monarch butterflies like to land in the same trees when they migrate.

(bkgd) Richard Ellis/Contributor/Getty Images News/Getty Images; (t, b) Don Farrall/Photographer's Choice RF/ Getty Images

There are more than 725 **species**, or kinds, of butterflies in the United States and Canada. These fascinating creatures taste leaves with their feet. They only see the colors yellow, red, and green. The Monarch butterfly and the Western Pygmy Blue butterfly share these traits. But they are also different in many ways.

SIZE AND COLOR

The Western Pygmy Blue butterfly is the smallest butterfly in the world. It is about a half-inch across. That's smaller than a dime! Monarch butterflies are much bigger. They are about four inches across.

Monarch butterflies are different from Pygmy Blues in other ways, too. Monarch butterflies are bright orange with black markings. Pygmy Blue butterflies are brown and blue.

This diagram shows the parts of a butterfly.

Western Pygmy Blue Butterfly

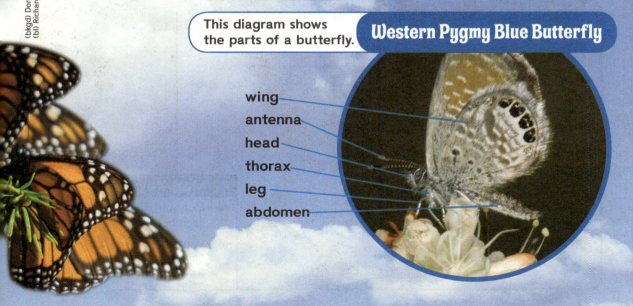

wing
antenna
head
thorax
leg
abdomen

(bkgd) Don Hammond/Design Pics; (t) Don Farrall/Photographer's Choice RF/Getty Images; (bl) Richard Ellis/Contributor/Getty Images News/Getty Images; (i) Charles Melton/Alamy

Text Evidence

1 Specific Vocabulary A C T

Read the word *species* in sentence one. Circle the word that means the same as *species*.

2 Sentence Structure A C T

Reread sentence two in the first paragraph. Circle the subject. Which noun in sentence one does the subject refer to? Underline the noun.

COLLABORATE

3 Talk About It

Describe how the Monarchs and Pygmy Blues are different in size.

Pygmy Blue butterflies are the

smallest _____

_____.

Monarch butterflies are _____

_____.

45

1 Specific Vocabulary A C T

Reread sentence one in the first paragraph. What words tell the meaning of the word *migrate*? Underline the words.

2 Comprehension
Compare and Contrast

Reread the second paragraph. How are Monarchs and Pygmy Blues alike? Circle the details that show you.

COLLABORATE

3 Talk About It

Discuss why has the Western Pygmy Blue population grown. Justify your answer.

The Western Pygmy Blue population has grown because

_____

_____ .

MOVING AROUND

Almost all butterflies **migrate**, or move to different areas. The Monarch migrates the longest distance of any butterfly. Many Monarchs travel more than 3,000 miles. Western Pygmy Blue butterflies migrate short distances.

Both Monarchs and Pygmy Blues migrate. Butterflies are cold-blooded insects. They are hot when the weather is hot. They are cold when the weather is cold. As a result, Monarch butterflies, which live in areas that get cold during winter, migrate south to stay warm. Western Pygmy Blues fly north to find food.

FINDING FOOD

The Western Pygmy Blue drinks the nectar of flowers. It easily finds the sweet, thick liquid, so its population has grown.

(bkgd) Don Hammond/Design Pics; (b) Mapping Specialists, Ltd.

This Western Pygmy Blue butterfly stops to eat.

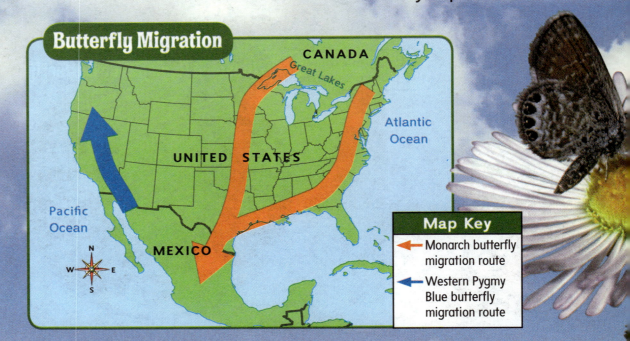

Butterfly Migration

CANADA
Great Lakes
UNITED STATES
Atlantic Ocean
Pacific Ocean
MEXICO
N W E S

Map Key
→ Monarch butterfly migration route
→ Western Pygmy Blue butterfly migration route

Both Pygmy Blue butterflies and Monarch butterflies sip nectar. But the Monarchs have one main food – the milkweed. They need this plant to live.

When people build houses and roads, there are fewer places for milkweed to grow. If the Monarch cannot find milkweed, its population will decrease.

HELP BUTTERFLIES

People need to **preserve** butterfly habitats. How can people help? They can work to change laws. They can plant milkweed. They can make it illegal to **destroy** animal habitats.

It is important to learn about butterflies and what they need to survive. People need to protect butterflies and their habitats. Then there will be many Western Pygmy Blue and Monarch butterflies in the **future**.

Monarch butterflies eat milkweed.

Make Connections

? How can people learn to respect butterflies? ESSENTIAL QUESTION

Talk about some butterflies you've seen. How are they alike and different? TEXT TO SELF

Text Evidence

1 Sentence Structure Ⓐ Ⓒ Ⓣ

Reread sentences two and three in paragraph one. Circle the pronoun *they*. Write the noun that *they* refers to.

_____

2 Specific Vocabulary Ⓐ Ⓒ Ⓣ

Reread sentence five in paragraph three. The word *destroy* means "to ruin." Which word in the paragraph means the opposite of *destroy*? Circle the word.

COLLABORATE

3 Talk About It

Discuss ways people can preserve butterfly habitats.

People can preserve butterfly

habitats by _____

_____

_____

47

Respond to the Text

Partner Discussion Work with a partner. Read the questions about "Butterflies Big and Small." Show where you found text evidence. Write the page numbers. Then discuss what you learned.

What did you learn about Monarch butterflies?

I read that Monarchs migrate from _____ to

_____.

In the text, Monarchs need to sip _____ from

_____.

Text Evidence 🔍

Page(s): _____

Page(s): _____

How can people respect butterflies?

People need to protect _____.

The text says people can plant _____.

I read that people can make laws that _____.

Text Evidence 🔍

Page(s): _____

Page(s): _____

Page(s): _____

Group Discussion Present your answers to the class. Cite text evidence for your ideas. Listen to and discuss the group's opinions.

Write Work with a partner. Look at your notes about "Butterflies Big and Small." Write your answer to the Essential Question. Use text evidence to support your answer. Use vocabulary words in your writing.

How does learning about the Monarch butterfly help you respect it?

Monarchs migrate from _____ to

_____.

Monarchs sip nectar _____ and need to have _____

_____.

People can protect _____ by _____

_____.

We need to respect _____ so that _____

_____.

Share Writing Present your writing to the class. Discuss their opinions. Think about their ideas. Explain why you agree or disagree. You can say:

I agree with _____.

That's a good comment, but _____.

Write to Sources

pages 44–47

Collin

Take Notes About the Text I took notes on this idea web to respond to the prompt: *Explain why Monarch butterflies migrate. Use evidence from the text.*

Monarchs are cold-blooded.

Monarch butterflies migrate to stay warm.

Monarchs fly from Canada to Mexico.

They are cold when the weather is cold.

Write About the Text I used notes to write about why Monarch butterflies migrate.

Student Model: *Informative Text*

Monarch butterflies migrate to stay warm. They start in Canada. They stop in Mexico. They migrate when it is cold. Monarchs are cold-blooded. They are hot when the weather is hot. They are cold when the weather is cold. So they fly to a warm place. Mexico is warmer than Canada. So the butterflies migrate more than 3,000 miles to stay warm!

TALK ABOUT IT

Text Evidence
Box the conclusion. Does this sentence retell Collin's main idea in different words?

Grammar
Underline the ninth sentence. **Circle** the adjective that compares the two countries.

Condense Ideas
Circle the second and third sentences. How can you condense the sentences to make one detailed sentence?

Your Turn

Compare the size and color of Monarch and Pygmy Blue butterflies. Include details from the text.

>> *Go Digital*
Write your response online. Use your editing checklist.

Weekly Concept   Funny Times

? **Essential Question**
What makes
you laugh?

>> *Go Digital*

COLLABORATE

What are the pigs doing? What other things make you laugh? Write the words in the web.

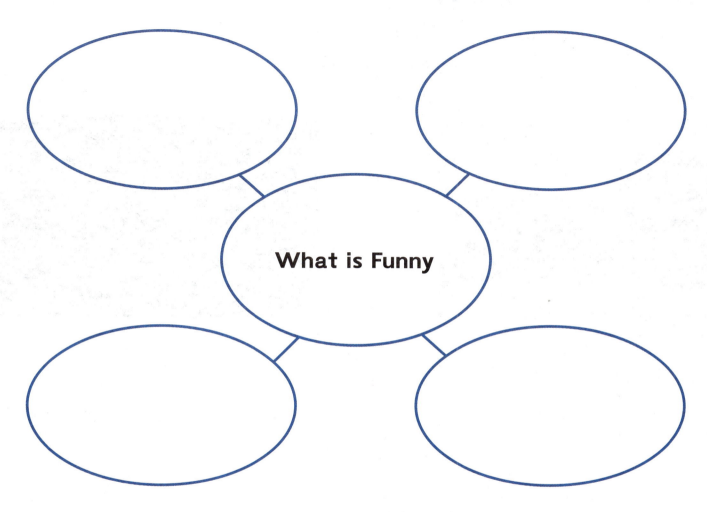

What is Funny

Why are the pigs funny? Talk about other things that make you laugh. Use the words from the web. You can say:

The pig looks like it is _____.

I like to tell _____ and make _____.

I laugh when I am _____ with my friends.

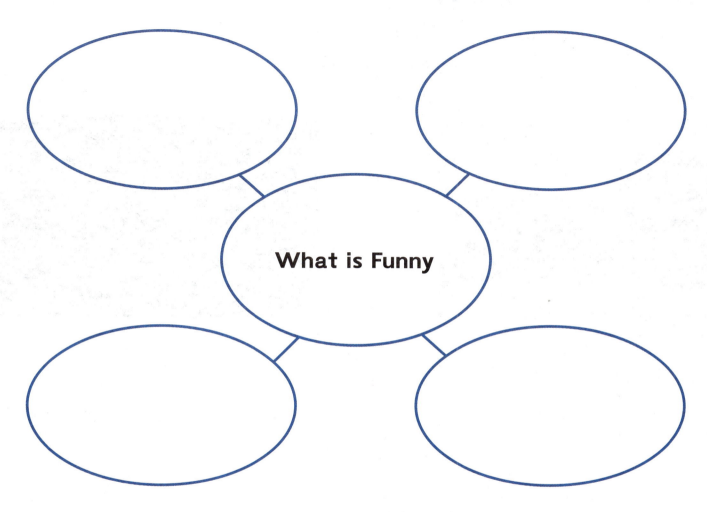 Bob Elsdale/Photonica/Getty Images

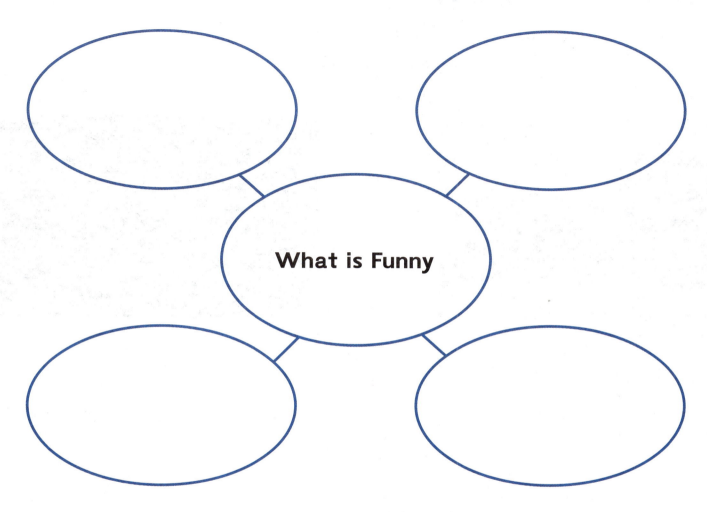 53

More Vocabulary

Look at the picture. Read the word. Then read the sentences.
Talk about the word with a partner. Answer the questions.

collapsed

The house **collapsed** during the storm.

Why did the house *collapse?*

_____

_____

_____

_____

slimy

This slug has **slimy** skin.

What slimy things have you seen?

_____

_____

_____

_____

Poetry Terms

rhyme

The words *moon* and *spoon* <mark>rhyme</mark>.
They end in the same sound.

The astronaut brought a spoon
On his trip to the Moon.

stanza

A <mark>stanza</mark> is a group of lines in a poem.
This stanza has two lines:

We roughed it at old Piney Park,
With tents and popcorn after dark.

COLLABORATE

Work with a partner. Make up a rhyme. Use the words below. Say the rhyme together.

leap   sleep   sheep

When I _____,

I dream of _____.

All night long I watch them _____.

COLLABORATE

❶ Talk About It

Read the title and look at the picture. Discuss what you see. Circle the words that tell you what the family is doing.

❷ Specific Vocabulary Ⓐ Ⓒ Ⓣ

Reread the first line. The phrase *roughed it* means "camped in a tent." Where does the narrator rough it? Write the place.

_____

_____

❸ Literary Element
Rhyme/Stanza

Look at the second stanza. Read it aloud. What word rhymes with *creep*? Write the word.

_____

_____

The Camping Trip

We **roughed it** at Old Piney Park,
With tents and hot dogs after dark.

I'd barely yawned and gone to sleep,
When I felt something creep, creep, creep.

A **slimy** something crawled on me,
Across my toe, up to my knee.

Essential Question

? **What makes you laugh?**

Read a poem about something funny.

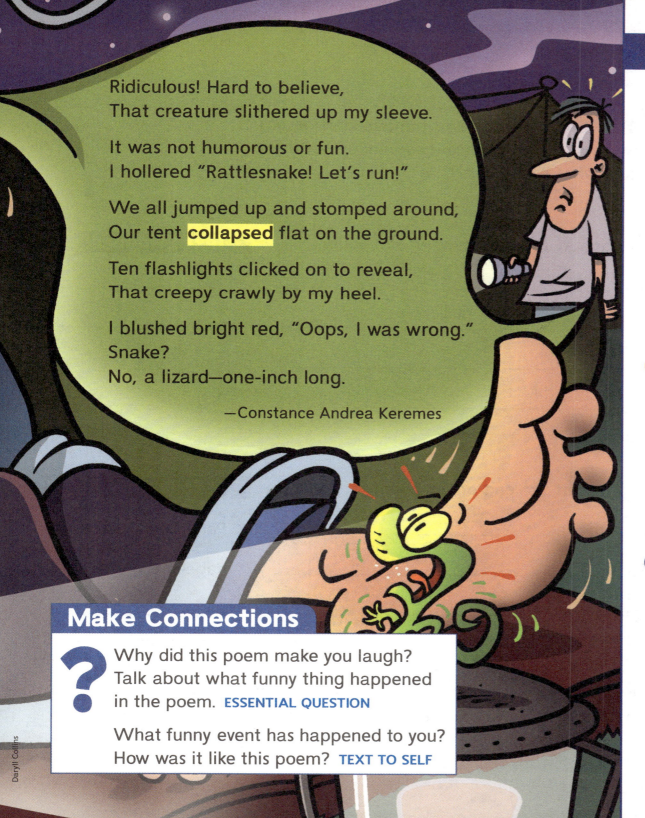

Ridiculous! Hard to believe,
That creature slithered up my sleeve.

It was not humorous or fun.
I hollered "Rattlesnake! Let's run!"

We all jumped up and stomped around,
Our tent **collapsed** flat on the ground.

Ten flashlights clicked on to reveal,
That creepy crawly by my heel.

I blushed bright red, "Oops, I was wrong."
Snake?
No, a lizard—one-inch long.

—Constance Andrea Keremes

Make Connections

? Why did this poem make you laugh? Talk about what funny thing happened in the poem. **ESSENTIAL QUESTION**

What funny event has happened to you? How was it like this poem? **TEXT TO SELF**

Daryll Collins

Text Evidence

❶ Comprehension
Point of View

Reread the second stanza. Look for clues that show how the narrator feels about the creature slithering. Write the words.

_____

_____

❷ Sentence Structure Ⓐ Ⓒ Ⓣ

Reread the fifth line. Circle the word that connects the two actions. Underline the two actions.

COLLABORATE
❸ Talk About It

How does the narrator feel at the end of the poem? Use text evidence. Discuss your answer.

The narrator feels _____

because _____

_____.

57

Respond to the Text

Partner Discussion Work with a partner. Read the questions about "The Camping Trip." Show where you found text evidence. Write the page numbers. Then discuss what you learned.

What is the funny situation at the beginning of the poem?

The campers rough it by _____.

Something _____ crawls on

_____.

It crawls up to _____.

Text Evidence 🔍

Page(s): _____

Page(s): _____

Page(s): _____

What is the funny situation at the end of the poem?

The boy thinks the creature is a _____.

The flashlights reveal _____.

The narrator is wrong because _____.

Text Evidence 🔍

Page(s): _____

Page(s): _____

Page(s): _____

Group Discussion Present your answers to the group. Cite text evidence for your ideas. Listen to and discuss the group's opinions.

Write Work with a partner. Look at your notes about "The Camping Trip." Write your answer to the Essential Question. Use text evidence to support your answer. Use vocabulary words in your writing.

What about this poem made you laugh?

When the narrator goes to sleep, he _____

_____.

After the campers jump up and stomp around, _____

_____.

The narrator blushes bright red because _____

_____.

Share Writing Present your writing to the class. Then talk about their opinions. Think about their ideas. Explain why you agree or disagree with their ideas. You can say:

I agree with _____.

That's a good comment, but _____.

Write to Sources

Jen

pages 56–57

Take Notes About the Text I took notes on this chart to answer the question: *How does the poet of "The Camping Trip" use rhyme in the stanzas of the poem?*

Stanza	Words that Rhyme
We roughed it at Old Piney Park, With tents and hot dogs after dark.	Park dark
A slimy something crawled on me, Across my toe, up to my knee.	me knee
We all jumped up and stomped around, Our tent collapsed flat on the ground.	around ground

Write About the Text I used notes to write about how the poet uses rhyme in the stanzas of the poem.

Student Model: *Informative Text*

The poet of "The Camping Trip" uses rhyme in each stanza. This poem has many stanzas. Each stanza has two lines. The last word of each line rhymes. The rhyming words end with the same sound. In the first stanza, the words "Park" and "dark" rhyme. In another stanza, the words "me" and "knee" rhyme. The poet uses two words that rhyme in each stanza.

TALK ABOUT IT

Text Evidence
Circle a pair of rhyming words that come from the chart. Why does Jen include these words in her explanation?

Grammar
Underline the prepositional phrase that tells where "Park" and "dark" are in the poem.

Connect Ideas
Draw a box around the second and third sentences. How can you combine the two sentences to connect the ideas?

Your Turn
Why is the poem funny? Use details from the text in your answer.

>> *Go Digital*
Write your response online. Use your editing checklist.